PASS THE NEW YORK NOTARY PUBLIC EXAM QUESTIONS AND ANSWERS

Angelo Tropea

ISBN 1449589677

Published by Angelo Tropea, P.O. Box 26271, Brooklyn, NY 11202-6271

Please note that laws relating to notaries public are available in many places, including online at:

http://public.leginfo.state.ny.us/menuf.cgi

Notaries Public…hold an office which can trace its origins back to ancient Rome when they were called *scribae, tabellius* or *notarius*. They are easily the oldest continuing branch of the legal profession worldwide.

Wikipedia.org

For information on acquiring the

Pass the New York Notary Public Exam

Computer Program

visit www.NotaryProgram.com

Additional information about this interactive computer software
which includes the sections of law specified for the notary public
exam may be found on page 173 of this book.

CONTENTS

THE AIM OF THIS BOOK

The NYS Department of State, Division of Licensing Services, has published an excellent booklet, "Notary Public License Law." It contains all the sections of law you need to pass the Notary Public Exam and to be a well informed and professional notary public. The aim of this book is to complement the official publication by highlighting the more important sections of law and offering study tools in the form of questions and answers on flash cards to help you better prepare for the exam and become a more knowledgeable and professional practicing notary public.

THIS BOOK PROVIDES:

1. True/False, fill-in and other "Quick Questions" to help you remember facts and definitions.

2. Multiple choice questions to help you practice for the notary public exam.

All the 225 questions are in flash card format – a popular and effective method of preparing for exams.

We believe that the combination of the above will provide the tools and the required practice to help you achieve your goal of passing the notary public exam and also increase your understanding and appreciation of laws important to notaries public.

For detailed information on how to apply for the NYS Notary Public Exam, please visit:

http://www.dos.state.ny.us/lcns/listoflncs.htm

HOW TO USE THIS BOOK

There are probably as many ways to study successfully as there are people. However, in the more than twenty-five years preparing study materials and conducting classes for civil service exams, I have found that certain methods seem to work better than others with the great majority of students. The following are time tested suggestions that you might want to consider as you incorporate this book in the study plan that is best for you.

SUGGESTIONS:

1. Try the "Quick Questions" first. Do not go on to the multiple choice questions until you have mastered these questions. Read the comments after each answer to reinforce important facts.

2. After the "Quick Questions" practice with the multiple choice questions. On the actual test you will have around 40 multiple choice questions.

Study every day. Take this book with you – and make it your friend.

In addition to the booklet that is available from the NYS Division of Licensing Services, the actual NYS statutes are available in many places, including online at:

http://public.leginfo.state.ny.us/menuf.cgi

NOTARY PUBLIC LAWS

The following is a list of laws relating to notaries public. The flash cards in this book are drawn from these statutes.

EXECUTIVE LAW

Section	Description and Page Number
130	Appointment of notaries public
131	Procedure of appointment; fees and commissions
132	Certificates of official character of notaries public
133	Certification of notarial signatures
134	Signature and seal of county clerk
135	Powers and duties, in general, of notaries public who are attorneys at law
135-a	Notary public or commissioner of deeds, acting without appointment, fraud in office
136	Notarial fees
137	Statement as to authority of notaries public
138	Powers of notaries public or other officers who are stockholders, directors, officers or employees of a corp.
140	(Appointment after removal from office)
142-a	Validity of acts of notaries public and commissioners of deeds notwithstanding certain defects

ELECTION LAW

3-200	(Election Commissioner)

PUBLIC OFFICERS LAW

3	(Selective draft acts)
10	Official oaths
67	Fees of Public Officers
69	Fee administering certain official oaths prohibited

REAL PROPERTY LAW

Section	Description and Page Number
290	Definitions and effect of article
298	Acknowledgments and proofs within the state
302	Acknowledgments and proofs by married women
303	Requisites of acknowledgments
304	Proof by subscribing witness
306	Certificate of acknowledgment of proof
309-a	Uniform forms of certificates of acknowledgment of proof within the state
309-b	Uniform forms of certificates of acknowledgment or proof without the state
330	Officers guilty of malfeasance liable for damages
333	Recording of conveyances of real property

JUDICIARY LAW

484	None but attorneys to practice in the state
485	Violation of certain preceding sections a misdemeanor
750	Power of courts to punish for criminal contempts

PENAL LAW

70.00	Sentence of imprisonment for felony
70.15	Sentences of imprisonment for misdemeanors and violations
170.10	Forgery in the second degree
175.40	Issuing a false certificate
195.00	Official misconduct

COUNTY LAW

534	County Clerk; appointments of notaries public

BANKING LAW

335	(Safe deposit boxes)

CIVIL PRACTICE LAW AND RULES

3113	(Persons before whom depositions may be taken

DOMESTIC RELATIONS LAW

11	(Marriages)

LEGAL TERMS

	(Acknowledgment to Will)

QUICK QUESTIONS
REMINDER

The flash cards in this book are not a replacement for reading the law. They are a study tool. After a careful review of the law, use the study cards (flash cards) to help you reinforce your understanding and memory of the law.

Study deep...

It will not only help you
pass the exam, but it will also help you
become a more knowledgeable,
respected and professional notary public!

QUESTION AND ANSWER FORMAT

Quick Questions are on pages which contain four questions each.

Each question is on a single card.

The answer to each question is on the following page.

In addition to the answer, there is more information.

For deeper understanding and retention, study both the answer and the additional information.

Multiple Choice Questions are on pages which contain two questions each.

Each question is on a single card.

The answer to each multiple choice question is on the following page.

In addition to the answer, there is more information.
For deeper understanding and retention, study both the answer and the additional information.

QUICK QUESTIONS

Executive Law 130: Appointment of notaries public

T/F? A notary at the time of appointment must be either a NYS resident or have a place of business in New York State.

Executive Law 130: Appointment of notaries public

T/F? A NYS resident notary public who moves out of NYS but still maintains a place of business in NYS can continue to be a notary in NYS.

Executive Law 130: Appointment of notaries public

T/F? In certain situations, the Secretary of State is not required to satisfy himself of certain notary public requirements of an applicant, such as education.

Executive Law 130: Appointment of notaries public

T/F? The Secretary of State can remove a notary without serving a copy of the charges against him.

QUICK ANSWERS

TRUE

A notary must also be a United States citizen at time of appointment (according to statute). However, the Department of State, Division of Licensing Services web site adds that a notary may also be a "permanent resident alien of the United States."

TRUE

However, if a non-resident notary ceases to have a place of business in NYS, then he vacates his office as a notary public.

TRUE

Example, when applicant applies less than 6 months after his term of notary has expired, or upon the application of an attorney admitted to practice in NYS, and certain court clerks.

FALSE

The Secretary of State must serve the charges and give him an opportunity to be heard.

QUICK QUESTIONS

Executive Law 130: Appointment of notaries public

T/F? No person shall be appointed a notary who has been convicted of any misdemeanor.

Executive Law 130: Appointment of notaries public

T/F? No person shall be appointed a notary public if he has been convicted of unlawful possession or distribution of habit forming narcotic drugs.

Executive Law 130: Appointment of notaries public

T/F? An attorney who is a notary public who moves to another state shall be deemed a resident of the county where he maintains an office in New York State.

Executive Law 131: Procedure of appointment; fees and commissions

T/F? The Secretary of State shall receive a fee of $20 for changing the name or address of a notary public.

QUICK ANSWERS

FALSE

A person cannot be appointed a notary if convicted of a FELONY.

TRUE

Also cannot be appointed a notary if convicted of vagrancy or prostitution (unless the person was subsequently pardoned or received a certificate of good conduct from a parole board).

TRUE

This section applies to attorneys who are admitted to practice in NYS and are counselors in the courts of record in New York State.

FALSE

The fee for changing the name or address of a notary public is $10. Also, the fee for issuing a duplicate I.D. (because of a lost card) is also $10.

QUICK QUESTIONS

Executive Law 132: Certificate of official character of notaries public

T/F? Only the Secretary of State may issue a Certificate of Official Character.

Executive Law 130: Appointment of notaries public

T/F? The Secretary of State shall collect $10 for the issuance of a Certificate of Official Character.

Executive Law 133: Certification of notarial signature

T/F? A certification of a notarial signature is issued by the court.

Executive Law 140:

T/F? No person removed from commissioner of deeds in New York City is eligible for reappointment as commissioner of deeds.

QUICK ANSWERS

FALSE

The county clerk may also issue a Certificate of Official Character.

TRUE

The county clerk collects $10 for the FILING of the Certificate of Official Character and $5 for the ISSUANCE of a Certificate of Official Character with seal attached.

FALSE

A certification of a notarial signature is issued by the county clerk for a fee of $3.

TRUE

Also not eligible for appointment as a notary public.

QUICK QUESTIONS

Election Law 3-200 and 3-400

T/F? A commissioner of elections or inspector of elections is not eligible for the office of notary public.

Public Officers Law 3

T/F? No person is eligible for the office of notary public who was convicted of a violation of the selective draft act of May 18, 1917.

County Law 534

T/F? There shall be at least one person in the county clerk's office who shall notarize documents for the public, free of charge.

Miscellaneous – Member of the legislature

T/F? A member of the legislature may not be appointed a notary public.

QUICK ANSWERS

FALSE

They are eligible for appointment as notary public.

TRUE

Also not eligible if convicted of a violation of the selective training and service act of 1940.

TRUE

That person shall be exempt from the notary public examination fee and application fee.

FALSE

A member of the legislature MAY be appointed a notary.

QUICK QUESTIONS

Miscellaneous – Sheriffs

T/F? A sheriff may be appointed notary public.

Notary Public – Disqualifications

T/F? A notary public shall not notarize a paper if he has a pecuniary interest in the transaction.

Executive Law 134: Signature and seal of county clerk

T/F? The signature and seal of the county clerk on a certificate of official character or authentication may be facsimile, printed or stamped.

Executive Law 135: Powers and duties

T/F? A notary shall not be liable to the parties injured for damages sustained by them as a result of the notary public's actions.

QUICK ANSWERS

FALSE

Sheriffs CANNOT hold any other office.

TRUE

Such notarization would be invalid.

TRUE

Also may be photographed or engraved thereon.

FALSE

A notary public IS liable for such damages.

QUICK QUESTIONS

Executive Law 135-a: Fraud, acting without appointment

T/F? A person not commissioned a notary public who acts as a notary public is guilty of a felony.

Executive Law 137: Statement as to authority of notaries public

T/F? A notary public who is licensed as an attorney in NYS may substitute the words "Attorney and Counselor at Law" for "Notary Public."

Executive Law 137: Statement as to authority of notaries public

T/F? No official act of a notary public shall be held invalid on account of failure to comply with the provisions listed in Executive Law 137.

Executive Law 138: Powers of notaries public

T/F? A notary public who is an employee or officer of a corporation may not take an acknowledgment of such corporation if the notary public has a financial interest in the instrument.

QUICK ANSWERS

FALSE

Such a person is guilty of a MISDEMEANOR. Also, fraud in office is also a misdemeanor (where not otherwise provided in this act.)

TRUE

Also, in NYC all notaries must affix to each instrument their official number.

TRUE

However, if such notary willfully fails to comply, he shall be subject to disciplinary action by the Secretary of State.

TRUE

Also, if the notary public is a director or agent of such corporation.

QUICK QUESTIONS

Executive Law 142-a: Validity of acts of notaries

T/F? An official certificate of a notary may be valid even if his term of office had expired.

Executive Law 142-a: Validity of acts of notaries

T/F? An official certificate of a notary may be valid even if there was an ineligibility of the notary to be appointed or commissioned.

Executive Law 142-a: Validity of acts of notaries

T/F? An official certificate of a notary may be valid even if the notary had vacated his office by changing his residence or accepting another public office.

Real Property Law 290: Definitions

T/F? The term "lien" includes every written instrument by which any estate or interest in real property is created, transferred, mortgaged or assigned.

QUICK ANSWERS

TRUE

Also valid if there is a misspelling or other error made in his appointment or commission.

TRUE

Also may be valid if there was an omission of the notary public to take or file his official oath.

TRUE

Also may be valid even if the action was taken outside the jurisdiction where the notary public was authorized to act..

FALSE

This definition applies to the legal term **"conveyance."**

QUICK QUESTIONS

Real Property Law 290: Definitions

T/F? The term "conveyance" does not include a will or a lease for a term not exceeding 3 years.

T/F? Real Property Law 298: Acknowledgments and proofs within the state

Acknowledgment or proof may be made before a justice of the peace within a county containing the town, village or city where he is authorized to perform official duties.

Real Property Law 302: Acknowledgments and proofs by married women

T/F? Acknowledgment or proof of conveyance of real estate within NYS or of any other written instrument may be made only by a married woman.

T/F? Real Property Law 304: Proof by subscribing witness

A subscribing witness must state his place of residence, but does not have to state that he knew or had satisfactory evidence of the identity of the person described in and who executed the instrument.

QUICK ANSWERS

TRUE

Also does not include an executor contract for the sale or purchase of lands.

TRUE

This applies also to town councilman, village police justice or judge of court of any inferior jurisdiction.

FALSE

It may be made by a single woman or a married woman.

FALSE

The subscribing witness MUST state that he knew the person described in and who executed the instrument or that he has satisfactory evidence that he is the same person who was a subscribing witness to the conveyance.

QUICK QUESTIONS

Real Property Law 306: Certificate of acknowledgment or proof

T/F? A person taking the acknowledgment or proof of a conveyance must endorse thereupon or attach a certificate signed by a county clerk.

Real Property Law 330: Malfeasance by officers

T/F? An officer who takes a proof of conveyance or other instrument who is guilty of malfeasance is not liable for damages to the person injured.

Real Property Law 333: When conveyances of real property not to be recorded

T/F? A conveyance of real property shall not be recorded unless it is in the English language.

Civil Practice Law and Rules 3113: Definitions

A deposition (may?/may not?) be taken before a notary public in a civil proceeding.

QUICK ANSWERS

FALSE

The certificate must be signed by the person taking the acknowledgment or proof

FALSE

He IS liable for damages to the person injured.

FALSE

MAY be recorded if there is attached to it an official translation proved and authenticated in a manner required of conveyances for recording in NYS.

A deposition MAY be taken before a notary public in a civil proceeding.

QUICK QUESTIONS

Banking Law 335: Safe deposit box

Within ____ days of the opening of the safe deposit box, a copy of the notary public's certificate must be mailed to the lessee at his last known postal address.

Domestic Relations Law 11: Marriage

A notary public (has?/does not have?) authority to solemnize marriages.

Public Officers Law 10: Official oaths

The oath of a public officer (may?/may not?) be administered by a notary public.

Judiciary Law 484: Practice by attorneys

T/F? A person can act as an attorney in New York State only if admitted to practice as an attorney or counselor in the courts of record in NYS.

QUICK ANSWERS

10 days.

Also, the box cannot be opened by the lessor until 30 days after notice to the lessee.

---

does NOT have

Also, a notary public may NOT take the acknowledgment of parties and witnesses to a written contract of marriage.

---

may

An oath to an official MAY be administered by a notary public.

TRUE

There is an exemption for the officers of societies for the prevention of cruelty and certain law students.

QUICK QUESTIONS

Judiciary Law 750: Wills

T/F? Notaries public are prohibited from executing wills because they would thereby be acting as an attorney.

Public Officers Law

T/F? A notary public is not a public officer.

Public Officers Law

A person who acts as a notary without having taken and duly filed the required oath of office is guilty of a _____.

Public Officers Law: Fees

T/F? A public officer cannot charge a fee, except where a fee or other compensation is expressly allowed by law.

QUICK ANSWERS

TRUE

Notaries public are expressly prohibited from drawing up wills.

FALSE

A notary public IS a public officer and must not act without having taken and duly filed the required oath of office.

---

misdemeanor

The oath must be as prescribed by law.

TRUE

Also, a public officer CANNOT charge more for the service than is allowed by law.

QUICK QUESTIONS

Public Officers Law: Fees

T/F? A public officer cannot receive a fee in advance of rendering the service.

Public Officers Law: Fees

T/F? An officer who violates the fee provisions is liable for treble damages to the person aggrieved.

Penal Law 70.00: Sentence of imprisonment for a felony

The maximum term of an indeterminate sentence shall be at least _____ years.

Penal Law 70.00: Sentence of imprisonment for a felony

For a class _____ felony, the term shall be fixed by the court and shall not exceed 7 years.

QUICK ANSWERS

FALSE

A public officer CAN receive a fee in advance IF the law allows. Also, cannot charge a fee unless the service was actually rendered by him.

TRUE

Also is liable for punishment prescribed by law for the criminal offense and removal from office.

3 years

The term is fixed by the judge.

"D"

Note that the maximum term of an indeterminate sentence shall be **at least** 3 years

QUICK QUESTIONS

Penal Law 70.15: Sentence of imprisonment for a misdemeanor

A sentence of imprisonment for a class "A" misdemeanor shall be a _____ sentence.

Penal Law 170.10: Forgery

A person is guilty of forgery in the _____ degree when he falsely makes, completes or alters a written instrument.

Penal Law 170.10: Forgery

Forgery in the second degree is a class ____ felony.

Penal Law 175.40: Issuing a false certificate

Issuing a false certificate is a class ____ felony.

QUICK ANSWERS

definite

Maximum jail for a misdemeanor is one year.

second

Examples: deed, will, codicil, contract, assignment, commercial instrument or public record or instrument.

"D"

This crime includes altering instruments officially issued or created by a public officer, public servant or governmental instrumentality.

"E"

A person is guilty if he issues such instrument knowing that it contains a false statement or false information.

QUICK QUESTIONS

Penal Law 195.00: Official misconduct

T/F? Official misconduct includes willfully committing an act relating to one's office constituting an unauthorized exercise of his official functions.

Penal Law 195.00: Notary officiating

T/F? An officer before whom an oath or affidavit may be taken is bound to administer the same when required.

Penal law: Perjury

A person is guilty of perjury if under oath or _____ he has given false testimony.

Definitions

An _____ is a formal declaration before an authorized officer by a person who has executed an instrument that such execution is his act and deed.

QUICK ANSWERS

TRUE

Also includes refraining from performing a duty which is imposed upon him by law or is clearly inherent in the nature of his office.

TRUE

Refusal to do so is a misdemeanor.

affirmation

The testimony must have been given on a material matter.

acknowledgment

The officer must know that the person making it is the person described and who executed the instrument.

QUICK QUESTIONS

Acknowledgments

T/F? It is not essential that the person who executed the instrument sign his name in the presence of the notary.

Acknowledgment

A notary who takes an acknowledgment over the telephone is guilty of a _____.

Acknowledgment

Unless the person who makes the acknowledgment appears in front of the notary, the notary's certificate that he so came is _____.

Certificates of acknowledgment

Making a false certificate is forgery in the _____ degree.

QUICK ANSWERS

TRUE

However, taking acknowledgments over the phone is illegal.

---

misdemeanor

However, it is not essential that the person sign in front of the notary.

---

fraudulent

However, it is not essential that the person who executed the instrument sign his name in the presence of the notary.

---

second

This is punishable by a term not exceeding 7 years.

QUICK QUESTIONS

Acknowledgment

A notary public (should?/should not?) take an acknowledgment to a legal instrument to which the notary is a party in interest.

Definitions

An (administrator?/affiant?) is a person appointed by the court to manage the estate of a deceased person who left no will.

Definitions

A (statute?/affidavit?) is a signed statement, duly sworn, before a notary public or other officer authorized to administer oaths.

Definitions

An (attestation?/apostile?) is a Department of State authentication attached to a notarized and county-certified document for international use.

QUICK ANSWERS

should not

A notary is liable for damages sustained due to a false certificate.

---

administrator

An affiant is a person who makes and subscribes his signature to an affidavit.

---

affidavit

A statute is a law established by an act of the legislature.

---

apostile

To attest is to witness the execution of a written instrument, at the request of the person who makes it, and subscribe the same as witness.

QUICK QUESTIONS

Definitions

An (authentication?/affirmation?) is a certificate attached by a county clerk to a certificate of proof or acknowledgment or oath signed by a notary.

Definitions

In an _____ _____ the witnesses certify that the instrument has been executed before them, and the manner of the execution of the same.

Definitions

An _____ is a solemn declaration made by persons who conscientiously decline taking an oath.

Definitions

A ___ __ ___ is a written instrument given to pass title of personal property from vendor to vendee.

QUICK ANSWERS

---

authentication

This county clerk's certificate authenticates or verifies the authority of the notary public to act as such.

---

attestation clause

Example: an attestation clause found at the end of a will.

---

affirmation

It is equivalent to an oath and just as binding.

---

bill of sale

Personal property, such as household goods and fixtures, is known as "chattel."

QUICK QUESTIONS

Definitions

_____ _____ is a writing or writings which evidence both an obligation to pay money and a security interest in specific goods.

Definitions

A _____ is an instrument made subsequent to a will and attached to the will.

Definitions

_____ is anything of value given to induce someone to enter into a contract.

Definitions

A ____ ____ is a copy of a public record signed and certified as a true copy by the public official having custody of the original.

QUICK ANSWERS

chattel paper

The agreement which creates or provides for the security interest is known as a security agreement.

codicil

The codicil adds to or modifies the will in some respects.

consideration

Consideration may be money, personal services, or even love and affection.

certified copy

A notary has NO authority to issue certified copies.

QUICK QUESTIONS

Definitions

Behavior that is disrespectful of the authority of a court which disrupts the execution of court orders is known as

_____ __ _____.

Definitions

A _____ is an agreement between competent parties to do or not do certain things for legal consideration.

Definitions

Generally, every instrument (except a will) by which any estate or interest in real property is created, transferred, assigned or surrendered is known as a _____.

Definitions

Another term for "County Clerk's Certificate" is _____.

QUICK ANSWERS

contempt of court

Contempt of court can be punished by the court.

contract

A contract can be written or oral.

conveyance

The instrument must be in writing.

authentication

Authentication (notarial).

QUICK QUESTIONS

Definitions

A _____ is one who makes an oath to a written statement.

Definitions

A _____ is the testimony of a witness taken out of court, before a notary or other person.

Definitions

Constraint exercised upon a person whereby he is forced to do some act against his will is known as _____.

Definitions

_____ is the placing of an instrument in the hands of a person as a depository who on the happening of an event must deliver it to a third person.

QUICK ANSWERS

deponent

A "deponent" is also known as an "affiant."

deposition

A deposition is intended to be used at the time of trial or hearing.

duress

The "constraint" must be "unlawful constraint."

escrow

The agreement should be unalterable.

QUICK QUESTIONS

Definitions

An _____ is one named in a will to carry out the provisions of the will.

Definitions

___ ___ means to do a hearing or examination in the presence of, or on papers filed by, one party in the absence of the other.

Definitions

A _____ is a crime punishable by death or imprisonment over one year.

Definitions

A _____ is a person in charge of a minor's person.

QUICK ANSWERS

executor

A will specifies the disposition of one's property to take effect after death.

ex parte

Ex parte means 'from one side only.'

felony

The imprisonment for a felony is in a state prison.

guardian

A guardian may also be in charge of a minor's property.

QUICK QUESTIONS

Definitions

A _____ is a decree of a court declaring that one party is indebted to another and fixing the amount of such indebtedness.

Executive Law 130: Appointment of notaries public

The _____ appoints and commissions notaries public in New York State.

Executive Law 130: Appointment of notaries public

The jurisdiction of notaries public is _____.

Executive Law 130: Appointment of notaries public

Notaries public are appointed for _____ years.

QUICK ANSWERS

judgment

A judgment can be for money or can determine the rights of parties.

Secretary of State

The Secretary of State appoints notaries for a 4 year term.

New York State (statewide)

(Notaries are appointed by the Secretary of State.)

4 years

At the end of that period they may apply to renew their term (reappointment).

QUICK QUESTIONS

Executive Law 130: Appointment of notaries public

Applications for notaries public are as prescribed by _____.

Executive Law 130: Appointment of notaries public

Attorneys and _____ are exempt from taking the notary public exam.

Executive Law 130: Appointment of notaries public

Applicants for notary public must have the equivalent of a _____ school education.

Executive Law 130: Appointment of notaries public

The _____ may suspend or remove a notary public from office.

QUICK ANSWERS

the Secretary of State

(The term of a notary public is 4 years.)

certain court clerks

(that work for the NYS Unified Court System and have been appointed as a result of a civil service exam in the Court Clerk series of exams.)

common school

Applicants must also be U.S. citizens at the time of appointment, as per Executive Law 130 (case law may differ).

Secretary of State

Grounds for removal include misconduct and fraud.

QUICK QUESTIONS

Executive Law 130: Appointment of notaries public

A person convicted of a _____ cannot be appointed a notary public.

Executive Law 130: Appointment of notaries public

A person convicted of unlawfully possessing or distributing habit forming narcotic drugs (can?/cannot?) be appointed a notary public.

Executive Law 130: Appointment of notaries public

T/F? A person sought to be removed as a notary public must be served a copy of the charges.

Executive Law 131: Procedure for appointment, fees and commissions

An oath of _____ shall be submitted to the Secretary of State with the application for notary public.

QUICK ANSWERS

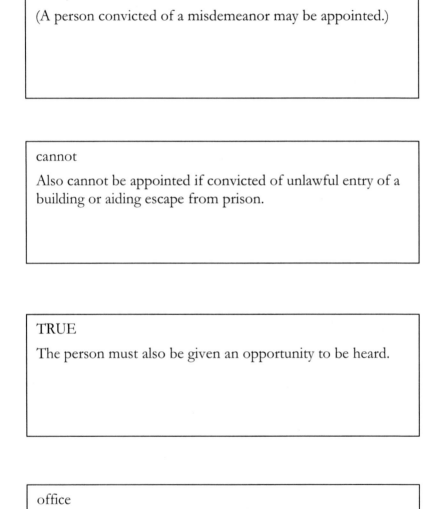

felony

(A person convicted of a misdemeanor may be appointed.)

cannot

Also cannot be appointed if convicted of unlawful entry of a building or aiding escape from prison.

TRUE

The person must also be given an opportunity to be heard.

office

Also, the oath must be duly executed before a person authorized to administer an oath.

QUICK QUESTIONS

Executive Law 131: Procedure for appointment, fees and commissions

The fee for notary public appointment is _____.

Executive Law 131: Procedure for appointment, fees and commissions

The notary public identification card contains the appointee's name, address, county and _____.

Executive Law 131: Procedure for appointment, fees and commissions

The Secretary of State must send $20 fee (apportioned from the $60 fee) to the _____ by the 10th day of the following month.

Executive Law 131: Procedure for appointment, fees and commissions (Application for reappointment)

The _____ makes an index of commissions and official signatures transmitted by the county clerk.

QUICK ANSWERS

$60

($20 of this amount is transmitted to the county clerk.)

commission term

(The commission term is for 4 years.)

county clerk

(Must also send a certified copy of the oath of office.)

Secretary of State

QUICK QUESTIONS

Executive Law 131: Procedure for appointment, fees and commissions (Reappointment)

The _____ issues reappointment commissions to notaries public.

Executive Law 131: Procedure for appointment, fees and commissions

The _____ shall receive a fee of $60 from each applicant for reappointment.

Executive Law 131: Procedure for appointment, fees and commissions

The county clerk shall transmit to the Secretary of State _____ from the fee for reappointment.

Executive Law 131: Procedure for appointment, fees and commissions

Generally, the Secretary of State shall receive a non-refundable fee of ____ for changing the name or address of a notary.

QUICK ANSWERS

county clerk

After issuing the commissions, the county clerk sends the list of commissions to the Secretary of State

county clerk

(Along with the $60 fee there must also be submitted by the notary public a reappointment application.)

$40

The fee must be submitted by the 10th of the following month.

$10

(Note that changes made in an application for reappointment do not require this fee.)

QUICK QUESTIONS

Executive Law 131: Procedure for appointment, fees and commissions

The Secretary of State may issue a duplicate identification card for a fee of ___.

Executive Law 132: Certificates of official character of notaries public

The county clerk where the notary commission is filed or the _____ may certify as to the official character of such notary public.

Executive Law 132: Certificates of official character of notaries public

The Secretary of State shall collect for a certificate of official character ISSUED by him the sum of $___.

Executive Law 132: Certificates of official character of notaries public

The county clerk charges a fee of $___ to FILE a certificate of official character.

QUICK ANSWERS

$10

(Each duplicate card must have stamped across its face the word "duplicate" and must have bear the same number as the one it replaces.)

Secretary of State

A notary public may file his autograph signature and a certificate of official character in the office of any county clerk in New York State.

$10

Also, the Secretary of State shall collect for a certificate of official character FILED by him the sum of $ $10.

$10

The county clerk charges a fee of $10 to FILE a certificate of official character (and $5 to ISSUE a certificate of official character).

QUICK QUESTIONS

Executive Law 132: Certificates of official character of notaries public

For each certificate of official character issued by a county clerk, a fee of $____ shall be collected by the county clerk.

Executive Law 140

A person removed from office as commissioner of deeds (is?/is not?) eligible to be appointed a notary public.

Executive Law 140

Acting as commissioner of deeds after removal is a ____ offense.

Election Law 3-200 and 3-400

A commissioner of elections (is?/is not/) eligible for the office of notary public.

QUICK ANSWERS

$5

For each certificate of official character ISSUED by a county clerk, a fee of $5 shall be collected by the county clerk.

IS NOT

Also, cannot be reappointed commissioner of deeds.

misdemeanor

(A misdemeanor offense is punishable with prison up to and including one year.)

IS

Also, an inspector of elections is eligible for the office of notary public.

QUICK QUESTIONS

Public Officers Law 3

A person convicted of a violation of the selective draft act of the U.S. (is?/is not/) eligible for appointment as notary public.

County Law 534

Each county clerk shall designate ay least ___ of his staff to act as notary public to notarize documents during business hours at no charge.

NYS Constitution, Article 13, Section 13(a)
A sheriff (may/?may not?) hold another office.

NYS Constitution, Article 3, Section 7
A member of the legislature (may?/may not?) be appointed a notary public.

QUICK ANSWERS

IS NOT

Also not eligible if convicted of violating amendments to the selective draft act.

one

The individual shall be exempt from the examination fee and the application fee.

MAY NOT

However, a member of the legislature MAY be a notary public.

MAY

A sheriff may not be appointed a notary public.

QUICK QUESTIONS

Case Law

A notary public who is pecuniarily interested in a transaction (is?/is not?) capable of acting as a notary public in that case.

Executive Law 134

T/F? The signature and seal of a county clerk on a certificate of authentication may be facsimile or printed.

Executive Law 135

T/F? Notaries public are empowered to administer oaths and affirmations.

Executive Law 135

T/F? Notaries cannot take affidavits and depositions.

QUICK ANSWERS

IS NOT

Also cannot do so if the notary is a party to the transaction.

TRUE

Signature may also be stamped, photographed or engraved.

TRUE

They are also empowered to take affidavits and depositions.

FALSE

They can also certify acknowledgments and proofs of deeds, mortgages and powers of attorney and other instruments.

QUICK QUESTIONS

Executive Law 135

T/F? Notaries can receive and certify acknowledgments or proofs of deeds, mortgages and powers of attorney and other instruments.

Executive Law 135

T/F? Notaries cannot demand acceptance or payment of foreign and inland bills of exchange.

Executive Law 135

T/F? Notaries can exercise powers and duties as by the laws of nations and according to commercial usage.

Executive Law 135

T/F? A notary who is an attorney may administer an oath or affirmation to his client in respect of any matter, claim, action or proceeding.

QUICK ANSWERS

TRUE

Notaries can also administer oaths and affirmations.

FALSE

Also, a notary can demand payment of promissory notes and obligations in writing.

TRUE

Notaries can exercise powers and duties as by the laws of nations and according to commercial usage or by the laws of any other government or country, provided that when exercising such powers the notary shall set forth the name of such other jurisdiction.

TRUE

Attorney must be admitted to practice in New York State.

QUICK QUESTIONS

Executive Law 135

T/F? A notary is not liable to parties injured for damages sustained by them.

Executive Law 135-a

A person who acts as a notary without first being appointed a notary is guilty of a _____.

Executive Law 135-a

A notary who practices fraud or deceit is guilty of a _____ offense.

Executive Law 136

A notary public is entitled to a fee of $____ for administering an oath or affirmation.

QUICK ANSWERS

FALSE

The notary IS liable for damages resulting from his misconduct.

---

misdemeanor

A misdemeanor is punishable with a jail term of up to and including a year.

---

misdemeanor

The notary is also liable for damages to the other parties.

$2

The fee may be different only when otherwise prescribed by law.

QUICK QUESTIONS

Executive Law 136

The fee for taking and certifying an acknowledgment or proof of execution of a written instrument is $_____.

Executive Law 142-a

T/F? An act or certificate of a notary is not made invalid due to the ineligibility of the notary public or commissioner of deeds to be appointed or commissioned.

Executive Law 142-a

T/F? An act or certificate of a notary is made invalid by a misnomer or misspelling of his name or other error made in his appointment or commission.

Executive Law 142-a

T/F? An act or certificate of a notary is made invalid by the expiration of the notary public's term, commission or appointment.

QUICK ANSWERS

$2
(for each person)

TRUE

There are exceptions, including where a person knew of the defect.

FALSE

Also NOT invalid if due to the expiration of his term.

FALSE

Also not invalid if due to misnomer or misspelling of name or other error made in his appointment or commission.

QUICK QUESTIONS

Executive Law 142-a

T/F? An act or certificate of a notary is not made invalid by the notary vacating his office by change of his residence, or by acceptance of another public office.

Executive Law 142-a

T/F? An act or certificate of a notary is not made invalid by the fact that the action was taken outside the jurisdiction where the notary public was authorized to act.

Real Property Law 298

T/F? The acknowledgment or proof WITHIN THE STATE of a conveyance of real property situated in NYS may be made at any place WITHIN THE STATE before a notary public, a justice of the supreme court, an official referee or an official examiner of title.

Real Property Law 298 T/F? The acknowledgment or proof WITHIN A DISTRICT may be made where any of the following officers are authorized to perform official duties: a judge of any court of record, commissioner of deeds, mayor or recorder of a city, a surrogate, county judge or the county clerk or other recording officer of a county.

QUICK ANSWERS

TRUE

and generally by any other action on his part.

TRUE

Same applies to commissioner of deeds.

TRUE

Note that the subject area is WITHIN THE STATE.

TRUE

Note that the subject area is WITHIN THE DISTRICT.

QUICK QUESTIONS

Real Property Law 298 T/F?

The acknowledgment or proof WITHIN A COUNTY may be made where any of the following officers are authorized to perform official duties: justice of peace, town councilman, village police justice, or a judge of any court of inferior local jurisdiction.

Real Property Law 302

The acknowledgment of a conveyance of real property within the state may be made by a married woman or _____ woman.

Real Property Law 303

T/F? An officer may take an acknowledgment even if he has no satisfactory evidence that the person making it is the person described in and who executed such instrument.

Real Property Law 304

When the execution of a conveyance is proved by a subscribing witness, such witness must state his _____ and that he knew the person described in and who executed the conveyance.

QUICK ANSWERS

TRUE

Note that the subject area is WITHIN A COUNTY.

---

unmarried

Married and unmarried women have the same rights.

FALSE

The officer MUST satisfy himself as to the identity of the person.

---

place of residence

and if the place of residence is in a city, must state his street and street number.

QUICK QUESTIONS

Real Property Law 333

T/F? Generally, for a record to be recorded it must be in the _____ language.

Real Property Law 333

T/F? If a record to be recorded is not in the English language, it must have attached a translation duly executed and acknowledged.

Banking Law 335

When a safe deposit box is opened as per this section, the notary public shall file with the lessor a certificate under seal which states the _____ of the safe deposit box and the name of the lessee.

Civil Practice Law and Rules 3113

T/F? In a civil proceeding a deposition may be taken before a notary public.

QUICK ANSWERS

English

Proper names may be in another language, but must be written in English characters.

TRUE

The translation must be by a person duly designated for such purpose by the county judge of the county where conveyance is to be recorded, or a justice of the supreme court.

date of opening

The certificate must also contain a list of the contents of the safe deposit box.

TRUE

Example: examination before trial (EBT)

QUICK QUESTIONS

Domestic Relations Law

T/F? A notary may solemnize a marriage.

Domestic Relations Law

A notary (may?/may not?) take the acknowledgment of parties and witnesses to a written contract of marriage.

Public Officers Law 10

T/F? A notary may administer an oath to a public officer.

Public Officers Law 750

A notary (may?/may not?) prepare a will.

QUICK ANSWERS

FALSE

Also, a notary cannot take the acknowledgment of parties and witnesses to a written contract of marriage.

may not

Also cannot solemnize a marriage.

TRUE

However, cannot charge a fee.

MAY NOT

This would constitute practicing law.

QUICK QUESTIONS

Public Officers Law 69

A notary (is entitled?/is not entitled?) to a fee for administering the oath of office to a member of the legislature, to any military office, to an inspector, or clerk of the poll.

Executive Law 135-a

T/F? A notary may be removed from office for making a misstatement of a material fact in his application for appointment.

Public Officers Law 15

T/F? A notary public is a public officer.

Penal Law 195

If a notary refrains from performing a duty imposed on him by law, he is guilty of official _____.

QUICK ANSWERS

IS NOT ENTITLED

Also not entitled to a fee for administering an oath to any other public officer or public employee.

TRUE

Also may be removed for misconduct and fraud.

TRUE

Because of this, a notary shall not execute any of the functions of his office without prior having taken and filed the required oath of office.

misconduct

Official misconduct is a class "A" misdemeanor.

MULTIPLE CHOICE QUESTIONS

Who commissions notaries public?

A. State Comptroller

B. County Clerks

C. Attorney General

D. Secretary of State

The application fee for a notary public commission is:

A. $40

B. $60

C. $80

D. $90

MULTIPLE CHOICE ANSWERS

D. Secretary of State

(Executive Law 130)

A record of the commissions is kept by the county clerk.

B. $60

(Schedule of Fees; Executive Law 130)

The Secretary of State keeps $40 and sends $20 to the county clerk where the appointee resides.

The county clerk makes an index of the commissions and official signatures transmitted to the county clerk by the Secretary of State.

MULTIPLE CHOICE QUESTIONS

An application for a notary public commission must be submitted to:

A. County Clerk.

B. Local civil court.

C. Division of Licensing Services.

D. None of the above.

Which of the following is correct?

An application for a notary public commission must include:

A. $45 filing fee.

B. a photograph of the applicant.

C. a copy of the applicant's social security card.

D. oath of office which must be sworn and notarized.

MULTIPLE CHOICE ANSWERS

C. Division of Licensing Services

(Executive Law 131)

The commission itself is issued by the Secretary of State

D. oath of office which must be sworn and notarized

(Executive Law 131)

The filing fee is $60, and NO copy of a social security card or photograph is required.

MULTIPLE CHOICE QUESTIONS

A "pass slip" showing that the applicant passed the notary public exam must be submitted along with:

A. application for citizenship.

B. application for a notary public commission.

C. application for a non driver state I.D.

D. None of the above.

Notary public examinations are regularly scheduled:

A. throughout NYS.

B. in NYC and Albany only.

C. only in counties with a population of over 1,000,000.

D. None of the above

MULTIPLE CHOICE ANSWERS

B. application for a notary public commission

(Division of licensing services booklet)

An applicant for a notary commission must submit to the Secretary of State:

1. $60 fee

2. application (includes oath of office)

A. throughout NYS

(Division of Licensing Services Booklet)

Also, notaries public are commissioned in their county of residence.

MULTIPLE CHOICE QUESTIONS

An individual who is an attorney:

A. cannot be a notary public.

B. can be a notary public if admitted to practice in NYS.

C. must be a notary public in all cases.

D. None of the above

The term of a commission of a notary public is _____.

A. 2 years

B. 4 years

C. 5 years

D. 6 years

MULTIPLE CHOICE ANSWERS

B. can be a notary public if admitted to practice in NYS.

(Executive Law 130)

Even if the attorney moves out of NYS, he can continue to act as a notary if he has a place of business within NYS.

B. 4 years

(Executive Law 130)

At the end of his term, a notary public can apply for reappointment.

MULTIPLE CHOICE QUESTIONS

Where are notaries public commissioned?

A. in their county of birth

B. in their city of preference

C. in their county of residence

D. None of the above

Which of the following is not correct?

After the Secretary of State approves an applicant for a notary public commission, he forwards the following to the appropriate county clerk:

A. the original oath of office

B. the signature of the notary public

C. the original social security card of the applicant

D. the notary public commission

MULTIPLE CHOICE ANSWERS

C. in their county of residence

(Executive Law 131)

If the notary does not reside in NYS, but has a place of business in NYS, then the county where he does business is considered his county of residence.

C. the original social security card of the applicant

(Executive Law 131)

The county clerk keeps an index of the commissions and official signatures sent to the county clerk by the Secretary of State.

MULTIPLE CHOICE QUESTIONS

Who maintains a record of the notaries public commissions and signatures?

A. the city comptroller

B. the county clerk

C. the Chief Clerk of the Supreme Court

D. None of the above

The public may obtain a certification of the notarial signature at the:

A. mayor's office

B. office of the attorney general

C. county clerk's office

D. None of the above

MULTIPLE CHOICE ANSWERS

B. the county clerk

(Executive Law 131)

The county clerk makes this index upon receipt of required information from the Secretary of State, and a $20 fee, by the 10th day of the following month.

C. county clerk's office

(Executive Law 131)

The fee for a certification of a notarial signature is $3.

MULTIPLE CHOICE QUESTIONS

If a non-resident attorney or person becomes a notary, the oath of office and signature must be filed in the office of the county clerk of the county where:

A. the attorney passed his bar exam.

B. the person or attorney live.

C. the office or place of business is located in NYS.

D. None of the above.

Acknowledgments and affidavits:

A. may not be taken over the phone.

B. may be taken over the phone if the affiant is ill.

C. may be taken over the phone if the affiant is a non-resident.

D. None of the above

MULTIPLE CHOICE ANSWERS

C. the office or place of business is located in NYS

(Division of Licensing Services Booklet)

Non-residents of NYS who are notaries are considered (deemed) to be residents of the county where their office or place of business is located.

A. may not be taken over the phone.

(Division of Licensing Services Booklet and case law)

In the Matter of Napolis, 169 App. Div. 469, 472, the court condemned the "acts of notaries taking acknowledgments or affidavits without the presence of the party whose acknowledgment is taken for the affiant."

MULTIPLE CHOICE QUESTIONS

Which of the following may be used when a person conscientiously declines to take an oath?

1. "Do you solemnly swear that the contents of this affidavit subscribed by you is correct and true?"

2. "Do you solemnly, sincerely and truly declare and affirm that the statements made by you are true and correct?"

A. 1 only is correct.

B. Both 1 and 2 are correct.

C. 2 only is correct.

D. Neither 1 nor 2 are correct.

Which of the following 4 statements is false? A notary public:

A. may not give advice on the law.

B. may not ask for and get legal business to refer to a lawyer with whom he has business or receives consideration for sending the business.

C. may agree to divide his fees with a lawyer.

D. may not advertise that he has powers not given to the notary by the laws under which the attorney was appointed.

MULTIPLE CHOICE ANSWERS

C. 2 only is correct.

(Division of Licensing Services Booklet and case law)

The statement must be made in front of an officer authorized to administer it.

C. May agree to divide his fees with a lawyer.

(Division of Licensing Services Booklet)

Making such an agreement would constitute practicing law, something which notaries are expressly prohibited from doing.

MULTIPLE CHOICE QUESTIONS

The jurisdiction of notaries public is:

A. the county of residence only.

B. the county of place of business only.

C. the city of residence or place of business only.

D. co-extensive with the boundaries of New York State.

Which of the following is false?

For a person to be appointed a notary public he must be:

A. a citizen of the United States

B. a resident of NYS or have a place of business in NYS.

C. a foreign national.

D. not convicted of a felony.

MULTIPLE CHOICE ANSWERS

D. co-extensive with the boundaries of New York State.

(Executive Law 130)

The jurisdiction of notaries appointed in any county in New York State is statewide.

C. a foreign national.

(Executive Law 130)

However, a person (US citizen) may reside out of NYS if he maintains an office in NYS.

MULTIPLE CHOICE QUESTIONS

Which of the following appears on a notary public identification card?

1. appointee's name and address

2. county and commission term

A. 1 only.

B. 2 only.

C. Both 1 and 2.

D. Neither 1 nor 2.

The commission and a certified copy or original oath of office and official signature, and $____ from the application fee shall be sent by the Secretary of State to the county clerk where the appointee resides by the ____ day of the following month.

A. $20....20th

B. $10....10th

C. $10....20th

D. $20....10th

MULTIPLE CHOICE ANSWERS

C. Both 1 and 2.

(Executive Law 131)

The I.D. card is sent to the appointee, and the commission and certified copy of the original oath of office and original signature and $20 is transmitted by the Secretary of State to the county clerk of the county of appointee's residence.

D. $20….10th

(Executive Law 131)

The Secretary of State retains $40 of the $60 application fee.

MULTIPLE CHOICE QUESTIONS

The county clerk collects a non-refundable application fee of $___ from each applicant for REAPPOINTMENT.

A. $20

B. $40

C. $60

D. $80

Except for changes made in a notary public's application for reappointment, the Secretary of State shall receive a fee of $____ for changing the name or address of the notary.

A. $10

B. $20

C. $30

D. $40

MULTIPLE CHOICE ANSWERS

C. $60

(Executive Law 131)

The county clerk then sends $40 of the $60 fee to the Secretary of State.

A. $10

(Executive Law 131)

The fee for issuing a duplicate I.D. card is also $10

MULTIPLE CHOICE QUESTIONS

The Secretary of State may issue a duplicate I.D. card to a notary to replace one that was lost, destroyed or damaged upon the payment of a fee of $____.

A. $60

B. $40

C. $20

D. $10

When the Secretary of State issues a certificate of official character, he must collect a fee of $____.

A. $5

B. $10

C. $20

D. $30

MULTIPLE CHOICE ANSWERS

D. $10

(Executive Law 131)

Each duplicate I.D. card must have the word "duplicate" stamped on it.

B. $10

(Executive Law 132)

The certificate of official character may also be ISSUED by the appropriate county clerk. The fee is $5.

(For FILING a certificate of official character with the county clerk, the fee is $10.)

MULTIPLE CHOICE QUESTIONS

For each certificate of official character issued by a county clerk, the sum of $____ shall be collected.

A. $5

B. $10

C. $20

D. $30

The fee for a certification of a notarial signature issued by a county clerk is $____.

A. $2

B. $3

C. $6

D. $10

MULTIPLE CHOICE ANSWERS

A. $5

(Executive Law 132)

Fee for the FILING with the county clerk of a certificate of official character is $10.

Fee for the ISSUANCE by the county clerk of a certificate of official character is $5.

B. $3

(Executive Law 133)

The certificate of authentication entitles the instrument to be read into evidence or recorded in any instance where a certificate is necessary for those purposes.

MULTIPLE CHOICE QUESTIONS

If a person who was removed from the office of commissioner of deeds (NYC) executes an instrument while posing as a commissioner of deeds, he shall be guilty of _____.

A. a violation

B. a felony

C. a misdemeanor

D. a petty offense

Which of the following two choices are correct?

The following persons are eligible for the office of notary public:

1. a commissioner of elections

2. an inspector of elections

A. Choice 1 only is correct.

B. Choice 2 only is correct.

C. Both choices 1 and 2 are correct.

D. Neither choice 1 nor choice 2 are correct.

MULTIPLE CHOICE ANSWERS

C. a misdemeanor

(Executive Law 140)

The same applies where the person poses as a notary.

C. Both choices 1 and 2 are correct.

(Election Law 3-200 and 3-400)

Also, a member of the legislature IS eligible.

A sheriff is NOT eligible.

MULTIPLE CHOICE QUESTIONS

Each county clerk must designate at least _____ employee(s) from his office to act as a notary public and notarize documents for the public for free.

A. one

B. two

C. three

D. four

Which of the following are eligible to be appointed notaries public?

1. a member of the legislature

2. a sheriff

A. 1 only is eligible for appointment.

B. 2 only is eligible for appointment.

C. Both 1 and 2 are eligible for appointment.

D. Neither 1 nor 2 are eligible for appointment.

MULTIPLE CHOICE ANSWERS

A. one

(County Law 534)

The individual(s) so appointed by the county clerk are exempt from paying the notary public application fee and notary public examination fee.

A. 1 only is eligible for appointment

(NYS Constitution, Article 3, Section 7 and
Article 13, Section 13(a))

Sheriffs are prohibited from holding any other office.

MULTIPLE CHOICE QUESTIONS

Which of the following are correct?

1. A notary public may be disqualified to act if he has an interest in the case.

2. A notary public interested in a conveyance is not competent to take the acknowledgment of an instrument.

A. 1 only is correct.

B. 2 only is correct.

C. Both 1 and 2 are correct.

D. Neither 1 nor 2 are correct.

Generally, a notary is entitled to a fee of $___ for administering an oath or affirmation and certifying the same when required.

A. $2

B. $4

C. $5

D. $6

MULTIPLE CHOICE ANSWERS

C. Both 1 and 2 are correct.

(Division of Licensing Services Booklet)

Generally, if a notary has a money interest in a case, then he is disqualified from acting as a notary in that case.

A. $2

(Executive Law 136)

The fee is $2 unless otherwise specifically prescribed by statute.

MULTIPLE CHOICE QUESTIONS

Generally, a notary is entitled to $___ for taking and certifying the acknowledgment or proof of execution of a written instrument (by one person). He is also entitled to $___ for each additional person and also $___ for swearing a witness thereto.

A. $2, $4, $6

B. $2, $2, $2

C. $4, $4, $4

D. None of the above.

A notary public who is duly licensed as an attorney and counselor at law in NYS may in his discretion substitute the following for the words "Notary Public."

A. Commissioner of NYS

B. Qualified Commissioner

C. Counselor at Law

D. None of the above

MULTIPLE CHOICE ANSWERS

B. $2, $2, $2

(Executive Law 136)

List of $2 fees:

Oath or affirmation / $2

Acknowledgment / $2 for each person

Swearing a witness / $ 2

Proof of execution / $2 (each person)

C. Counselor at Law

(Executive Law 137)

The attorney must be duly licensed as an attorney and counselor at law in New York State.

MULTIPLE CHOICE QUESTIONS

Which of the following is the best answer?

Section 142-a of the Executive Law states that an act of a notary or commissioner of deeds is valid even if:

A. the notary was not eligible to be appointed.

B. there existed a misspelling or other error made in the appointment of the notary.

C. the term of the notary had expired.

D. All of the above are correct.

Which of the following three choices are correct?

The term "conveyance" includes:

1. a written instrument by which an estate in real property is created.

2. a written instrument which effects title to real property.

3. a will.

A. 1 only is correct.

B. 1 and 2 only are correct.

C. 1, 2 and 3 are all correct.

D. 2 only is correct.

MULTIPLE CHOICE ANSWERS

D. All of the above are correct.

(Executive Law 142-a)

Also valid if notary had vacated his office because of a change in his residence, or if the notary acted outside the jurisdiction where he was authorized to act.

B. 1 and 2 only are correct.

(Real Property Law 290)

"Conveyance" also includes a written instrument by which an estate in real property is transferred, assigned or mortgaged.

MULTIPLE CHOICE QUESTIONS

The acknowledgment or proof within NYS of a conveyance of real property in NYS may be made AT ANY PLACE WITHIN THE STATE, before:

1. a justice of the supreme court

2. an official examiner of title or an official referee

3. a notary public

A. Only 1 and 3 are correct.

B. Only 2 and 3 are correct.

C. 1, 2 and 3 are all correct.

D. Only 3 is correct.

The acknowledgment or proof, within the state, of a conveyance of real property in NYS may be made WITHIN THE DISTRICT where the officer is authorized before:

1. the mayor or recorder of a city

2. commissioner of deeds, judge or clerk of any court of record

3. county clerk or other recording officer of the county.

A. 1, 2 and 3 are correct.

B. Only 1 and 2 are correct.

C. Only 2 and 3 are correct.

D. Only 3 is correct.

MULTIPLE CHOICE ANSWERS

C. 1, 2 and 3 are all correct.

(Property Law 298)

Note the difference between the choices in this question and the choices in the following question. The difference is in the GEOGRAPHICAL AREA OF NYS where the acknowledgment may be made. The jurisdiction of the listed officials is different. It varies from statewide to local.

A. 1, 2 and 3 are correct.

(Property Law 298)

Note the difference between the choices in this question and the choices in the previous question. The difference is in the GEOGRAPHICAL AREA OF NYS where the acknowledgment may be made. The jurisdiction of the listed officials is different. It varies from statewide to local.

MULTIPLE CHOICE QUESTIONS

Which of the following fees is not correct?

A. Appointment as Notary Public fee (total) / $60

B. Change of Name/Address / $20

C. Duplicate Identification Card / $10

D. Issuance of Certificate of Official Character / $5

Which of the following fees is not correct?

A. Filing Certificate of Official Character / $10

B. Authentication Certificate / $3

C. Protest of Note, Commercial Paper, etc. / $.75

D. Oath or Affirmation / $4

MULTIPLE CHOICE ANSWERS

B. Change of Name/Address / $20

(Schedule of Fees)

The correct fee for Change of Name/Address is $10

D. Oath or Affirmation / $4

(Schedule of Fees)

The correct fee for Oath or Affirmation is $2

MULTIPLE CHOICE QUESTIONS

Which of the following fees is not correct?

A. Acknowledgment (each person) / $2

B. Proof of Execution (each person) / $2

C. Swearing Witness / $2

D. Duplicate Identification Card / $20

A declaration before a duly authorized officer by a person who has executed an instrument that the execution is his act is known as _____.

A. a conveyance

B. a jurat

C. an affiant

D. an acknowledgment

MULTIPLE CHOICE ANSWERS

D. Duplicate Identification Card / $20

(Schedule of Fees)

The fee for a duplicate identification card is / $10

D. an acknowledgment

(Definitions)

The term acknowledgment is also used to mean the certificate of an officer who is authorized to take an acknowledgment of the conveyance of real property.

MULTIPLE CHOICE QUESTIONS

Someone appointed by a court to manage the affairs (estate) of a person who died without a will is known as _____.

A. a plaintiff

B. an affiant

C. an administrator

D. an executor

A person who signs an affidavit is called _____.

A. an administrator

B. an affiant

C. a jurat

D. an executor

MULTIPLE CHOICE ANSWERS

C. an administrator

(Definitions)

If the person dies with a will and names in the will the person to manage his affairs, then that person is called the executor.

B. an affiant

(Definitions)

The affiant can either affirm or swear (take an oath).

MULTIPLE CHOICE QUESTIONS

Personal property (not real property) is also called _____.

A. codicil

B. apostile

C. escrow

D. chattel

A written instrument (except a will) used to create, transfer, surrender or assign an interest in real property is called _____.

A. a conveyance

B. a deposition

C. a jurat

D. an affirmation

MULTIPLE CHOICE ANSWERS

D. chattel

(Definitions)

Examples of personal property are clothing, cars, jewelry, etc.

A. a conveyance

(Definitions)

An example is a deed.

MULTIPLE CHOICE QUESTIONS

The authentication attached by the Department of State to a notarized document that is county-certified for possible international use is called _____.

A. a lien

B. a codicil

C. an apostile

D. an affirmation

A _____ is an instrument attached to a will that adds to or modifies the will.

A. judgment

B. apostile

C. chattel

D. codicil

MULTIPLE CHOICE ANSWERS

C. an apostile

(Definitions)

The document in question:

1. is notarized

2. is county-certified

3. contains the apostile (attached)

D. codicil

(Definitions)

The codicil is created after the creation of the will.

MULTIPLE CHOICE QUESTIONS

A(n) _____ is a person who is named in a will to carry out the will's provisions.

A. deponent

B. executor

C. jurat

D. affiant

A crime (other than a felony) is called _____.

A. a violation

B. a "C" misdemeanor

C. a petty offense

D. a misdemeanor

MULTIPLE CHOICE ANSWERS

B. executor

(Definitions)

If there is no will or no one is named in the will, then the court appoints an administrator.

D. a misdemeanor

(Definitions)

A crime is either a misdemeanor or a felony.

MULTIPLE CHOICE QUESTIONS

A _____ is a decree of a court which declares the amount of money which one party owes to another party.

A. apostile

B. judgment

C. jurat

D. codicil

A _____ is a claim or right to property which attaches to the specific property until a judgment (debt) is paid.

A. lien

B. conveyance

C. laches

D. chattel

MULTIPLE CHOICE ANSWERS

B. judgment

(Definitions)

A judgment can be final or temporary.

A. lien

(Definitions)

Liens may be filed at the county clerk's office.

MULTIPLE CHOICE QUESTIONS

The term _____ can be used interchangeably with "affiant."

A. litigator

B. guardian

C. deponent

D. juror

A verbal pledge by a person that his statements are true is known as an _____.

A. apostile

B. oath

C. authentication

D. lien

MULTIPLE CHOICE ANSWERS

C. deponent

(Definitions)

The deponent swears an oath to a written statement or "affirms."

B. oath

(Definitions)

An oath cannot be administered over the telephone and must be done in a manner in accordance with statute.

MULTIPLE CHOICE QUESTIONS

A person who starts a civil action is called _____.

A. the defendant

B. the appellant

C. the plaintiff

D. the guardian

A written statement called _____ empowers a person to act for another person.

A. an authentication

B. an affirmation

C. an ex parte instrument

D. a power of attorney

MULTIPLE CHOICE ANSWERS

C. the plaintiff

(Definitions)

The person that the plaintiff sues is called the defendant.

D. a power of attorney

(Definitions)

The person designated can act for the other person but does not have the right to practice law.

MULTIPLE CHOICE QUESTIONS

The statute which prescribes the period during which a civil action or criminal prosecution may be started is the _____.

A. statute of frauds

B. statute of minorities

C. statute of limitations

D. None of the above.

A person who is legally in charge of the property of a minor person or legally in charge of the minor person's property is called _____.

A. a defendant

B. a juror

C. a plaintiff

D. a guardian

MULTIPLE CHOICE ANSWERS

C. statute of limitations

(Definitions)

If a case is not started within the prescribed period, then the case may be dismissed.

D. a guardian

(Definitions)

Guardians may also be appointed for people that are mentally or physically incapacitated.

MULTIPLE CHOICE QUESTIONS

Something of value (Example: chattel, personal services, money, etc.) given to induce someone to enter into a contract is called _____.

A. a deponent

B. a will

C. an affirmation

D. consideration

Which of the following statements is not correct?

A. Notaries are appointed by the Secretary of State.

B. The jurisdiction of notaries is the entire New York State.

C. Notaries are appointed for a 2 year term.

D. Notaries at time of appointment must be U.S. citizens.

MULTIPLE CHOICE ANSWERS

D. consideration

(Definitions)

Services and affection are also consideration.

C. Notaries are appointed for a 2 year term.

(Executive Law 130)

Notaries are appointed for a 4 year term.

MULTIPLE CHOICE QUESTIONS

A non-resident of NYS who accepts the office of NYS notary appoints the _____ as the person on whom process can be served in his behalf.

A. State Comptroller

B. Governor

C. Lieutenant Governor

D. Secretary of State

Which of the following choices is false?

The Secretary of State must satisfy himself that notary public applicants:

A. are of good moral character

B. have the equivalent of a common school education.

C. are familiar with duties and responsibilities of notary publics.

D. have a college education.

MULTIPLE CHOICE ANSWERS

D. Secretary of State

(Executive Law 130)

The Secretary of State also examines the qualifications of applicants for notary public.

D. have a college education.

(Executive Law 130)

Also, the education requirement does not apply when applicants are attorneys or certain court clerks.

MULTIPLE CHOICE QUESTIONS

Which of the following choices is false?

No person can be appointed a notary public if he has been convicted of any of the following:

A. illegally using, carrying or possessing a pistol.

B. making or possessing burglar's instruments.

C. entry of a building.

D. aiding escape from prison.

Notary public applicants must submit to _____ the application, oath of office, and their signature.

A. clerk of court

B. Secretary of State

C. State Comptroller

D. Attorney General of NYS

MULTIPLE CHOICE ANSWERS

C. entry of a building.

(Executive Law 130)

UNLAWFUL entry of a building.

B. Secretary of State

(Executive Law 131)

The officer who issues the notary public commission is the Secretary of State.

MULTIPLE CHOICE QUESTIONS

The Secretary of State shall receive a non-refundable application fee of $_____ from applicants for appointment.

A. $20

B. $40

C. $60

D. $90

A notary public I.D. card must indicate the appointee's name, address, county and _____.

A. social security number

B. commission term

C. date of birth

D. gender

MULTIPLE CHOICE ANSWERS

C. $60

(Executive Law 131)

No further fee has to be paid for the issuance of the notary public commission.

B. commission term

(Executive Law 131)

The fee for the issuance of a duplicate card is $10.

MULTIPLE CHOICE QUESTIONS

Which of the following choices is false?

The Secretary of State must submit to the county clerk where the appointee resides the following:

A. the commission, duly dated

B. certified copy or original oath of office

C. the official signature

D. $30 apportioned from the application fee.

Applicants for reappointment shall submit to _____ their application and oath of office and $60 fee.

A. the clerk of court

B. the Secretary of State

C. the county clerk

D. Attorney General

MULTIPLE CHOICE ANSWERS

D. $30 apportioned from the application fee.

(Executive Law 131)

The correct amount is $20.

C. the county clerk

(Executive Law 131)

The county clerk must send $40 to the Secretary of State.

MULTIPLE CHOICE QUESTIONS

Which of the following choices is the best answer?

An instrument with an authentication of the notarial signature shall:

A. be entitled to be read into evidence.

B. be entitled to be recorded in any county of NYS.

C. both A and B

D. Neither A nor B

A person removed from office of notary public who signs or executes an instrument as notary is guilty of_____.

A. a violation

B. a misdemeanor

C. a felony

D. an "A" felony

MULTIPLE CHOICE ANSWERS

C. both A and B

(Executive Law 133)

Note that the county clerk authenticates the signature on the basis of the certification of the signature that was filed.

B. a misdemeanor

(Executive Law 140)

Same applies for a person removed as commissioner of deeds.

MULTIPLE CHOICE QUESTIONS

Which of the following choices is false?

A notary public is authorized to:

A. administer oaths and affirmations.

B. take affidavits and depositions.

C. receive and certify acknowledgments or proofs of deeds.

D. act as a sheriff.

Generally, a notary public is entitled to the following fee for administering an oath and certifying the same:

A. $2

B. $4

C. $6

D. $12

MULTIPLE CHOICE ANSWERS

D. act as a sheriff.

(Executive Law 135)

Also, a notary public who is an attorney may administer an oath or affirmation to his client.

A. $2

(Executive Law 136)

Also, $2 for certifying an acknowledgment or proof of execution of a written instrument ($2 for one person, $2 for each additional person, $2 for swearing in each witness)

MULTIPLE CHOICE QUESTIONS

Which of the following is not correct?

A notary public shall print, write or stamp beneath his signature in black ink:

A. his name.

B. the words "Notary Public State of New York"

C. the name of the county in which he originally qualified.

D. his date of birth.

Which of the following statements is false?

Acknowledgment or proof within NYS of a conveyance of real property situated in NYS may be made anywhere in NYS before:

A. a justice of the supreme court.

B. an official examiner of title.

C. a notary public.

D. any municipal official.

MULTIPLE CHOICE ANSWERS

D. his date of birth.

(Executive Law 137)

Must write the date his **commission** expires.

D. any municipal official.

(Real Property Law 298)

Can also be made before an official referee.

MULTIPLE CHOICE QUESTIONS

Select the best answer:

An acknowledgment **within a district** where an officer is authorized to perform his official duties may be made before:

A. a judge, clerk of court, or mayor or recorder of a city only.

B. surrogate, special surrogate, or special county judge only.

C. county clerk or other recording officer of a county only.

D. A, B and C are all correct.

Choose the best answer:

An acknowledgment shall not be taken by any officer unless he knows or has satisfactory evidence that:

A. the person making it is the person described.

B. the person is the person who executed such instrument.

C. Neither A nor B are correct.

D. Both A and B are correct.

MULTIPLE CHOICE ANSWERS

D. A, B and C are all correct.

(Real Property Law 298)

May be made also before a commissioner of deeds (outside NYC) or commissioner of deed (within NYC).

D. Both A and B are correct.

(Real Property Law 303)

The notary must know the person or have satisfactory evidence as to the identity of the person.

MULTIPLE CHOICE QUESTIONS

Which of the following choices would be correct fill-ins in the following: "On the _____ day of ___ in the year _____."

A. Wednesday...week...2009

B. afternoon...April...2009

C. 6ᵗʰ...June...2009

D. last...the month...2008

Which of the following choices is most correct?

When authorized, a notary public shall be present when a safe deposit box is opened by the lessor. The notary public shall file with the lessor a certificate which states:

A. the date of the opening of the safe deposit box.

B. a list of the contents.

C. Both A and B are correct.

D. Neither A nor B are correct.

MULTIPLE CHOICE ANSWERS

C. 6th...June...2009
(Real Property Law 309)

Same applies to certificate of proof of execution by a subscribing witness.

C. Both A and B are correct.
(Banking Law 335)

The certificate must contain:

1) the date of opening of the safe deposit box,

2) the name of the lessee, and

3) a list of the contents.

MULTIPLE CHOICE QUESTIONS

A person who violates the provisions of Judiciary Law 484 (Practicing as an attorney) shall be guilty of _____.

A. a violation

B. a misdemeanor

C. An "E" felony

D. a "B" felony

Which of the following statements is false?

An officer is not entitled to a fee for administering an oath to:

A. a teacher or college professor.

B. a member of the legislature.

C. to any military officer.

D. to an inspector of elections.

MULTIPLE CHOICE ANSWERS

B. a misdemeanor

(Judiciary Law 485)

Examples of such acts are the notary public presenting himself as an attorney or preparing wills, codicils, or pleadings of any kind.

A. a teacher or college professor.

(Public Officers Law)

Also, cannot collect a fee from a clerk of the poll, or from any public officer or public employee while in the performance of their duties.

MULTIPLE CHOICE QUESTIONS

Which of the following choices is the best answer?

A notary may be removed from office for:

A. practicing fraud or deceit.

B. making a misstatement of a material fact in the application for appointment.

C. Both A and B are correct.

D. Neither A nor B are correct.

A notary public in exercising his powers under this article must in addition to the venue and signature print, typewrite, or stamp beneath his signature in _____ ink, his name, the words "Notary Public State of New York," the name of the county in which he originally qualified and date upon which his commission expires.

A. blue (only)

B. black (only)

C. black or blue

D. black, blue or green

MULTIPLE CHOICE ANSWERS

C. Both A and B are correct.

(Executive Law)

Also may be removed for preparing and taking an oath of an affiant to a statement the notary knew to be false or fraudulent.

B. black (only)

(Executive Law 137)

MULTIPLE CHOICE QUESTIONS

Which of the following statements is false?

A. A guardian is a person in charge of a minor's person or property.

B. A felony is a crime that is punishable by imprisonment over one year or death.

C. Duress is forcing a person against his will to do something by exercising unlawful constraint on that person.

D. An administrator is a person named in a will to carry out the provisions in the will.

Which of the following statements is false?

A. Statutes are laws that are passed by a legislature.

B. A plaintiff is the person who commences a civil lawsuit.

C. An apostile is an authentication by the Department of State.

D. Chattel is real property.

MULTIPLE CHOICE ANSWERS

D

(Legal Terms)

An **executor** is a person named in a will to carry out the provisions in the will.

D

(Legal Terms)

Chattel is **personal** property.

PASS THE NOTARY EXAM - NEW YORK STATE
COMPUTER PROGRAM

This new computer program contains all of the questions in this book, along with interactive features which make learning both easy and fun! The program is designed to be fast and simple.

It includes a 'Quick Program Tour' which displays all the screens in the program, including the 'Home Page Screen' which has 6 buttons to take you to the 6 parts of the program.

The "Notary Exam' button explains the Notary Exam..

The 'Quick Questions' button takes you to hundreds of T/F Questions where you can practice with interactive flash cards.

The 'Multiple choice screen provides extra practice. The multiple choice questions will make you think hard and remember better. It has a review feature for any questions you answer incorrectly.

The program also remembers the Quick Questions that you answer incorrectly so that you may review them in 'My Difficult Questions' section. This encourages you to study the questions that you find difficult. Once the program determines that you are answering a difficult question correctly, it will remove it from the 'My Difficult Questions' section.

FAST AND EASY AND FUN!

You can download the program and start using this valuable tool immediately or you can order the CD by mail.

Either way, you will be pleasantly surprised by its ease of use and effectiveness. Learn more about this inexpensive and helpful study tool at:

www.NotaryProgram.com

LaVergne, TN USA
30 January 2011
214588LV00004B/96/P